I HAVE A DREAM

I HAVE
A DREAM

MARTIN LUTHER KING, JR.

Foreword by Rev. Bernice A. King

HarperSanFrancisco
A Division of HarperCollins*Publishers*

Disclaimer: The words that appear here are the original words written by Martin Luther King Jr., and are slightly different from the words Reverend King spoke on August 28, 1963.

I HAVE A DREAM. Copyright © 1963, 1993, by Coretta Scott King, Yolanda Denise King, Martin Luther King, III, Dexter Scott King, and Bernice Albertine King. Foreword by Reverend Bernice Albertine King. Copyright © 1993 by Bernice Albertine King. All rights reserved. Printed in the United States of America. No part of this book may be used or reproduced in any manner whatsoever without written permission except in the case of brief quotations embodied in critical articles and reviews. For information address HarperCollins Publishers, 10 East 53rd Street, New York, NY 10022.

Photos copyright Flip Schulke

FIRST EDITION

Library of Congress Cataloging-in-Publication Data
King, Martin Luther, Jr., 1929–1968.
   I have a dream / Martin Luther King, Jr.—1st ed.
     p. cm.
   ISBN 0–06–250947–0 (cloth : alk. paper)
   1. Afro-Americans—Civil rights. 2. Civil rights movements—United States—History—20th century. 3. March on Washington for Jobs and Freedom, Washington, D.C., 1963. I. Title.
E185.97.K5A5 1993
323.1'196073—dc20   93–24727
                                        CIP

93 94 95 96 97 ❖ HAD 10 9 8 7 6 5 4 3 2 1

This edition is printed on acid-free paper that meets the American National Standards Institute Z39.48 Standard.

FOREWORD

Titles can have a way of misleading people. Certainly this has been the case with the "I Have a Dream" speech by my father, Martin Luther King, Jr. While it is the most well-known, and most often quoted speech by Dr. King, it is also the most misunderstood. Too often people have hallowed the portion beginning with "I Have a Dream" without giving any credence to the portion that precedes it. In a real sense, though, "I Have a Dream" is the sweetener that Dr. King mixed in to enhance the flavor of his message.

For indeed, the circumstances out of which the message emerged were a bitter reality for the victims of social and economic injustice. And so, the "I Have a Dream" speech is really a message of hope, whose effect was to comfort the disturbed, but not without disturbing the comfortable.

In the following pages, you will read this message of hope given by Martin Luther King, Jr., on August 28, 1963, at the historic March on Washington. I encourage you to remove any blinders that would prohibit you from experiencing the full essence of it, for there is a lot to be gained, even thirty years later. The same injustices continue to threaten life in America. Just as those who heeded the message then were able to keep striving for freedom, justice, and equality, the same message calls out to those who are willing to continue the quest to overcome the injustices of the day. After reading this message of hope, *may you be inspired to keep striving*

for the promised land.

x
~

REVEREND BERNICE A. KING

APRIL 1993

I Have a Dream

March on Washington, August 28, 1963. The crowd as viewed from the Lincoln Memorial. Photograph © Flip Schulke.

I AM HAPPY to join with you today in what will go down in history as the greatest demonstration for freedom in the history of our nation.

Fivescore years ago, a great American, in whose symbolic shadow we stand today, signed the Emancipation Proclamation. This momentous decree came as a great beacon light of hope to millions of Negro slaves who had been seared in the flames of withering injustice. It came as a joyous daybreak to end the long night of their captivity.

But one hundred years later, the Negro still is not free; one hundred years later, the life of the Negro is still sadly crippled by the manacles of segregation and the chains of discrimination; one hundred years later, the Negro lives on a lonely island of poverty in the midst of a vast ocean of material prosperity; one hundred years later, the Negro is still languished in the corners of American society and finds himself in exile in his own land.

So we've come here today to dramatize a shameful condition. In a sense we've come to our nation's capital to cash a check. When the architects of our republic wrote the magnificent words of the Constitution and the

Declaration of Independence, they were signing a promissory note to which every American was to fall heir. This note was the promise that all men, yes, black men as well as white men, would be guaranteed the unalienable rights of life, liberty, and the pursuit of happiness.

5

It is obvious today that America has defaulted on this promissory note insofar as her citizens of color are concerned. Instead of honoring this sacred obligation, America has given the Negro people a bad check; a check which has come back marked "insufficient funds." We refuse to believe that there are insufficient funds in the great vaults of opportunity of this nation. And so we've come to cash this check, a check that will give us upon demand the riches of freedom and the security of justice.

We have also come to this hallowed spot to remind America of the

7

8

fierce urgency of now. This is no time
to engage in the luxury of cooling off
or to take the tranquilizing drug of
gradualism. Now is the time to make
real the promises of democracy; now is
the time to rise from the dark and des-
olate valley of segregation to the sunlit
path of racial justice; now is the time

to lift our nation from the quicksands of racial injustice to the solid rock of brotherhood; now is the time to make justice a reality for all God's children. It would be fatal for the nation to overlook the urgency of the moment. This sweltering summer of the Negro's legitimate discontent will not pass until there is an invigorating autumn of freedom and equality.

10

Nineteen sixty-three is not an end, but a beginning. And those who hope that the Negro needed to blow off steam and will now be content, will have a rude awakening if the nation returns to business as usual.

There will be neither rest nor tranquility in America until the Negro is granted his citizenship rights. The whirlwinds of revolt will continue to shake the foundations of our nation until the bright day of justice emerges.

But there is something that I must say to my people who stand on the warm threshold which leads into the palace of justice. In the process of gaining our rightful place we must not be guilty of wrongful deeds.

Let us not seek to satisfy our thirst for freedom by drinking from the cup of bitterness and hatred. We must forever conduct our struggle on

the high plane of dignity and disci-
pline. We must not allow our creative
protest to degenerate into physical vio-
lence. Again and again we must rise to
the majestic heights of meeting physical force with soul force.

The marvelous new militancy
which has engulfed the Negro commu-

14

nity must not lead us to a distrust of all white people, for many of our white brothers, as evidenced by their presence here today, have come to realize that their destiny is tied up with our destiny and they have come to realize that their freedom is inextricably bound to our freedom. This offense we share mounted to storm the battlements of injustice must be carried forth by a biracial army. We cannot walk alone.

15

And as we walk, we must make the pledge that we shall always march ahead. We cannot turn back. There are those who are asking the devotees of civil rights, "When will you be satisfied?" We can never be satisfied as long as the Negro is the victim of the unspeakable horrors of police brutality.

We can never be satisfied as long as our bodies, heavy with fatigue of travel, cannot gain lodging in the motels of the highways and the hotels of the cities. We cannot be satisfied as long as the Negro's basic mobility is from a smaller ghetto to a larger one.

We can never be satisfied as long as our children are stripped of their selfhood and robbed of their dignity by signs stating "for whites only." We cannot be satisfied as long as a Negro in Mississippi cannot vote and a

Negro in New York believes he has nothing for which to vote. No, we are not satisfied, and we will not be satisfied until justice rolls down like waters and righteousness like a mighty stream.

I am not unmindful that some of you come here out of excessive trials and tribulation. Some of you have come fresh from narrow jail cells. Some of you have come from areas where your quest for freedom left you battered by the storms of persecution and staggered by the winds of police brutality. You have been the veterans of creative suffering. Continue to work

19

with the faith that unearned suffering
is redemptive.

Go back to Mississippi; go back
to Alabama; go back to South Car-
olina; go back to Georgia; go back to
Louisiana; go back to the slums and
ghettos of the northern cities, knowing
that somehow this situation can, and

will, be changed. Let us not wallow in the valley of despair.

So I say to you, my friends, that even though we must face the difficulties of today and tomorrow, I still have a dream. It is a dream deeply rooted in the American dream that one day this nation will rise up and live out the true meaning of its creed—we hold these truths to be self-evident, that all men are created equal.

I have a dream that one day on the red hills of Georgia, sons of former slaves and sons of former slave-owners will be able to sit down together at the table of brotherhood.

I have a dream that one day, even the state of Mississippi, a state sweltering with the heat of injustice, sweltering with the heat of oppression, will be transformed into an oasis of freedom and justice.

I have a dream my four little children will one day live in a nation where they will not be judged by the color of their skin but by the content of their character. I have a dream today!

I have a dream that one day, down in Alabama, with its vicious racists, with its governor having his lips dripping with the words of interposition and nullification, that one day, right there in Alabama, little black boys and black girls will be able to join hands with little white boys and white girls as sisters and brothers. I have a dream today!

I have a dream that one day every valley shall be exalted, every hill and mountain shall be made low, the rough places shall be made plain, and the crooked places shall be made straight and the glory of the Lord will be revealed and all flesh shall see it together.

This is our hope. This is the faith that I go back to the South with.

With this faith we will be able
to hew out of the mountain of despair
a stone of hope. With this faith we
will be able to transform the jangling
discords of our nation into a beautiful
symphony of brotherhood.

With this faith we will be able
to work together, to pray together,

to struggle together, to go to jail together, to stand up for freedom together, knowing that we will be free one day. This will be the day when all of God's children will be able to sing with new meaning—"my country 'tis of thee; sweet land of liberty; of thee I sing; land where my fathers died, land of the pilgrim's pride; from every mountain side, let freedom ring"—and if America is to be a great nation, this must become true.

So let freedom ring from the prodigious hilltops of New Hampshire.

Let freedom ring from the mighty mountains of New York.

Let freedom ring from the heightening Alleghenies of Pennsylvania.

Let freedom ring from the snowcapped Rockies of Colorado.

Let freedom ring from the curvaceous slopes of California.

But not only that.

Let freedom ring from Stone Mountain of Georgia.

Let freedom ring from Lookout Mountain of Tennessee.

Let freedom ring from every hill and molehill of Mississippi, from every mountainside, let freedom ring.

And when we allow freedom

to ring, when we let it ring from every village and hamlet, from every state and city, we will be able to speed up that day when all of God's children—black men and white men, Jews and Gentiles, Catholics and Protestants—will be able to join hands and to sing in the words of the old

Negro spiritual, "Free at last, free at last; thank God Almighty, we are free at last."